What Was the Age of Exploration?

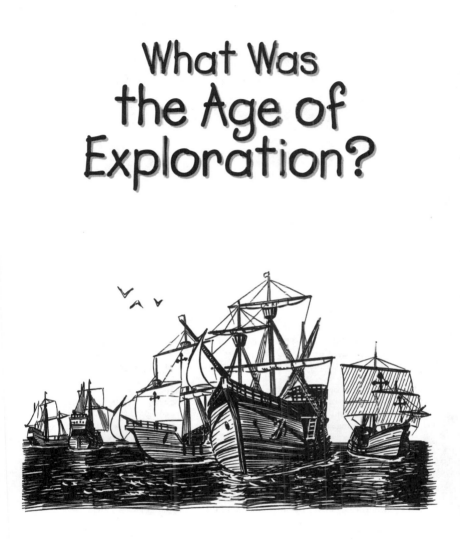

by Catherine Daly

illustrated by Jake Murray

Penguin Workshop

With love to Jon and Oonagh—CD

PENGUIN WORKSHOP
An Imprint of Penguin Random House LLC, New York

Visit us online at www.penguinrandomhouse.com.

Library of Congress Cataloging-in-Publication Data is available upon request.

ISBN 9780593093825 (paperback)   10 9 8 7 6 5 4 3 2 1
ISBN 9780593093832 (library binding)   10 9 8 7 6 5 4 3 2 1

Contents

What Was the Age of Exploration? 1

Marco Polo and the Silk Road 6

Portugal Leads the Way 15

The Slave Trade Begins 23

A New Player: Christopher Columbus . . . 28

Things Get Spicy for Portugal 58

All the Way Around the Globe 65

A New Kind of Explorer 79

The Inca 89

The Search for the Northwest Passage . . . 94

The Age of Exploration: A Lasting Impact . . 102

Timelines 104

Bibliography 106

What Was the Age of Exploration?

The island of Hispaniola
(present-day Dominican Republic and Haiti)

The man was inside a barrel. He had to stay quiet and still. The barrel was going to be loaded onto a ship sailing to South America, to a place called Urabá (now Colombia).

Why couldn't the man board the ship like the rest of the crew? He owed a lot of money to people in Hispaniola, and they wouldn't let him leave. So he had to find a way to sneak off the island. Hiding inside a barrel was the answer.

The man's name was Vasco Núñez de Balboa (say: VAS-co NOO-nyez day bal-BOH-uh), and the year was 1510. Balboa could hear other barrels being rolled aboard. At last it was his turn.

His plan worked! The barrel he was inside of hit the deck.

When the ship was finally at sea, Balboa got out of his barrel. The captain was angry. But then he learned that Balboa was a Spanish explorer who had already been to Urabá. He would be useful once they arrived. So the captain didn't throw Balboa overboard.

When the ship reached Urabá, there was a horrible surprise. The Spanish colony had nearly been wiped out by the local Native people. So Balboa suggested that the ship should instead head to the Isthmus of Panama. (An isthmus is a narrow strip of land with water on either side.) He knew that the Native people there were friendly to Europeans. Balboa also hoped he and the other Spanish explorers would discover gold there. The settlement was named Santa María de la Antigua del Darién.

In 1513, Balboa set off with hundreds of Native people and about 190 Spaniards, including Francisco Pizarro, who was also to become a famous explorer. Their journey took nearly a month. There were mountains, swamps, and thick rain forests to navigate. They encountered alligators, poisonous snakes, swarms of mosquitoes, and cannibals. Many men died along the way. Finally, they reached the other side of the isthmus. Balboa climbed to the top of a mountain and took a look.

Did Balboa find gold? No. Instead, he found himself gazing upon a vast sea that no European had ever seen before. Balboa put on his armor, waded into the waves, and claimed the ocean for Spain. He named it the South Sea (now the Pacific Ocean).

Did Balboa discover the Pacific Ocean? Absolutely not. And he had no right to "claim it" for Spain. European explorers, however, felt entitled to do this.

Balboa's story did not have a happy ending. His enemies had him falsely arrested, accusing him of betraying his country. Pizarro turned on him. Balboa was beheaded in 1519, and his head was stuck on a spike for all to see.

Balboa was just one of a number of European explorers who—from the 1400s into the 1600s—ventured beyond the lands familiar to them. Many did not survive. Through their voyages, however, they completely changed what people knew about the world. We call this time the Age of Exploration.

CHAPTER 1
Marco Polo and the Silk Road

Like many people today, wealthy Europeans of long ago liked fancy things. And a lot of the fancy things they liked—ivory, jewels, and silks, among others—came from the Indies. (That was the name Europeans in the Middle Ages used for Asia and India.) In addition, Europeans wanted spices that were not grown in their homelands.

While finding and selling these goods could make traders rich, the trip from Europe to the Indies was long, difficult, and dangerous.

Until the end of the 1400s, there were two ways to reach the Indies from Europe. One was by sea, a journey called the Spice Route. A ship had to cross the Mediterranean Sea on its way to the Middle East, then sail around India through Indonesia and

The Spice Route

on to China. Just sailing across the Mediterranean was difficult. The powerful city-state of Venice controlled the route and often stopped ships from going any farther or taxed them heavily to proceed.

Spices

Why did the Europeans want spices so badly? Spices were an important part of daily life. They were used for medicine. Also for creating perfume and cosmetics. Because there were no refrigerators, spices were used to keep food from spoiling. And if the food did happen to go bad, spices could help hide the unpleasant taste.

Another way to the Indies was by land, following the Silk Road. It was a series of roads covering four thousand miles, passing through vast deserts and over steep mountains. The Silk Road connected Europe and Asia. Most people didn't travel the whole distance. There were trading posts along the way where European merchants could stop. They could buy or trade goods and then return home to sell them.

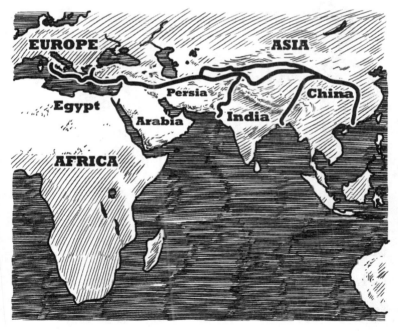

The Silk Road

For those who did make the entire journey, it took years to travel from Europe to Asia and back. This made the price of goods expensive when they were sold back home.

In 1271, a teenager from Venice named Marco Polo convinced his father and uncle, both wealthy merchants, to allow him to join their

trip along the Silk Road to Cathay (now China). It took three and a half years to get there, crossing seas, deserts, and mountains while also encountering thieves and wars, and suffering illnesses. It is believed that when once in Cathay, the Polos became friends with the emperor, Kublai Khan. (The elder Polos had first met him on an earlier trip.)

Marco was amazed by what he saw in Cathay. There were golden palaces, dazzling silks, glittering jewels, bountiful spices, and animals he had never seen before, including elephants and monkeys. The Polos were able to explore many parts of Asia that no European had been to. They spent twenty-four years away from home. When

Kublai Khan

the three men returned to Venice in 1295, their family and friends were shocked to discover that they were still alive—and weighed down with jewels.

At the time of the Polos' return, Venice was at war over the spice trade with another city-state, Genoa. Marco Polo fought for Venice and was captured and imprisoned for one year.

Camels, the Ships of the Desert

How did merchants like the Polos survive a trip across the Takla Makan and Gobi Deserts? On the back of a camel, of course! Camels can easily carry hundreds of pounds of goods—much more weight than horses or donkeys can haul. They can go without water for as long as two weeks, and for several months without food because of the fat they store in their humps. There's one thing to watch out for, however—when a camel feels threatened, it spits vomit!

In prison, he met an author named Rustichello, who wrote down everything that Marco Polo told him about Cathay. All this was turned into a book in about 1350. *The Travels of Marco Polo* became a best seller. It inspired several future explorers, including Vasco da Gama and Christopher Columbus.

Certainly, there was great wealth to be made by trading with Asia. But there needed to be an easier, quicker way to get there than by following the Spice Route or the Silk Road.

The question was *how* to do so.

Was It True?

Some of the details in *The Travels of Marco Polo* are untrue, including an island inhabited by dog-faced people. Even back then, people mocked some of Marco's stories. Later, some questioned if Marco Polo even went to China. For instance, it is odd that he never mentions chopsticks. And there is no mention of him or his father or uncle in any Chinese accounts during all the years the

Polos were said to be in China. But on his deathbed, Marco Polo insisted that he had told only half of what he had seen during his travels there.

CHAPTER 2
Portugal Leads the Way

One person with a great interest in finding a new route to the Indies was Prince Henry of Portugal, born in 1394. According to his horoscope (a horoscope is a foretelling of your  future based on the way the stars, planets, sun, and moon were positioned in the sky when you were born), Prince Henry was going to dedicate his life to great and noble conquests. He wanted to do everything possible to make this prediction come true.

As a young man, Prince Henry and his family

led a crusade (a religious war) against a Muslim town on the North African coast. It was named Ceuta. The town was a center for trading—spices from the Indies, jewels, and precious metals.

From that time, Prince Henry became interested in finding another route to the Far East, one that would go all the way around Africa and then on to Asia. Finding a sea route would cut out Venetian and Muslim middlemen. The cost of spices would go way down.

Sailing around Africa would not be easy. No European explorers had ever gone beyond Cape Bojador. It was on the stormy western coast of Africa where the sea was shallow. Sailors thought it was too dangerous to venture any farther than there.

That was not going to stop Prince Henry. In addition to getting rich, he had another reason for exploring the coast of Africa. He was a devout Christian. He hoped that Portuguese ships would make stops all along the coast and convert African people to his religion. (To convert means to change to a new religion.)

Muslim Traders

The Venetians controlled the Mediterranean Sea, and Muslim traders controlled the spice supply. (Muslims follow the religion called Islam. It was founded in Mecca, now in Saudi Arabia, in the seventh century by a prophet named Muhammad.) The Muslim traders would travel to India and the Spice Islands—a group of islands in what is now Indonesia. To scare off others from going themselves, Venetians told tales of terrible snakes and other dangerous creatures that guarded the spices.

So it was a prince from the tiny country of Portugal who started the Age of Exploration. And although he did not go on any of the voyages, he became known as Henry the Navigator because he paid for so many. (Navigators are expert sailors able to find their way to remote destinations.)

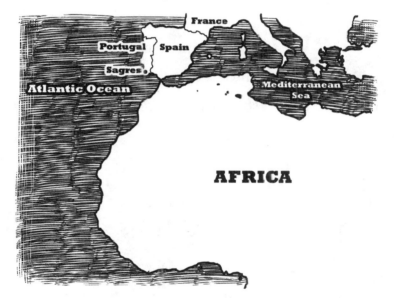

In 1419, Prince Henry moved to the southwestern-most tip of Portugal. The place was called Sagres. It was the perfect spot from which to set sail for Africa.

In Sagres, he brought together the best navigators, mapmakers, astronomers and ship-builders. They improved many of the instruments that sailors relied on, such as the astrolabe and quadrant. Both were used to locate the position of the stars, sun, and moon to help figure out where a ship was. There was also a better compass by then.

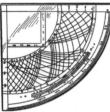

Astrolabe

Quadrant

Carrack

Another improvement was the caravel, a new kind of ship. The caravel was smaller and simpler to sail than the carrack, an earlier type of ship.

Caravel

It had triangular sails that made it easier to sail into the wind. The ship was also faster, cutting down the time for long trips. The sails also made it easier to turn the ship faster when navigating rocky coasts.

The maps sailors used were old and inaccurate. Prince Henry wanted new ones. So he had cartographers (mapmakers) gather information from diaries written by captains on recent voyages. Diaries like these are called logs.

Fourteen times, Prince Henry sent ships out to go past Cape Bojador. All met with failure. Finally, in 1434, he sent out a Portuguese sailor named Gil Eanes to try yet again. And this time, his sailor made it!

This opened up the western coast of Africa for further exploration. But it would be more than fifty years before anyone would make it around the bottom of the continent, and up the eastern coast.

CHAPTER 3
The Slave Trade Begins

Many Portuguese people thought Prince Henry was spending too much on explorations without seeing any return on the money. But that soon changed.

The riches didn't come from spices or jewels, however. They came from the sale of human beings. In 1444, Gil Eanes returned from the West African coast with two hundred prisoners. These enslaved people were brought to Lagos, Portugal, where they were sold off. Prince Henry went on to build a slavery trading post in Northern Africa, off the coast of what is now Mauritania. Slavery had almost always existed before this. But now it became a booming business.

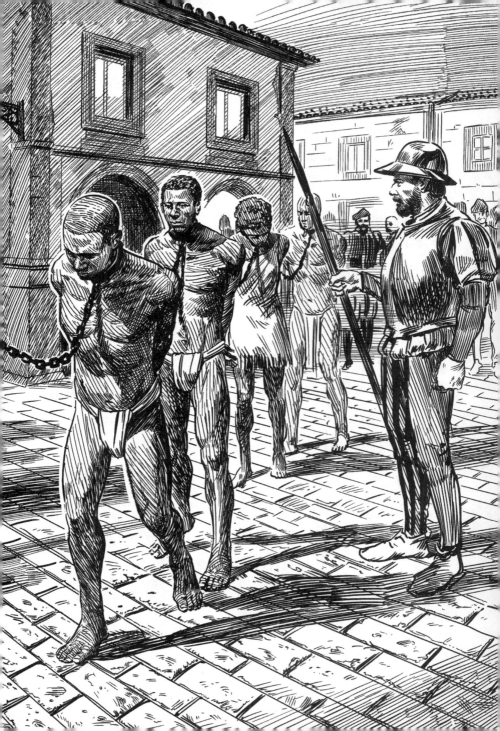

The need for a route around Africa to the Indies became even more urgent in 1453. That was because the Ottoman Turks had conquered Constantinople (present-day Istanbul). That city had been an important starting point for following the Silk Road. Now it was closed off to Europeans.

Prince Henry died in 1460. By then, his explorations had gotten as far as Sierra Leone, western Africa, about a thousand nautical miles past Cape Bojador. Twenty-one years later, his nephew became king. Like his uncle, King John II wanted to continue exploration to the Indies. In 1487, he sent out three ships, with Bartholomeu Dias in charge (say: bahr-THOL-uh-may-yoo DEE-az). The expedition was to go way

Bartholomeu Dias

past Cape Bojador. King John II wanted the ships to sail all the way around Africa.

There were several reasons why navigating around the tip of the continent was so hard. Besides the rough waters, there were tricky currents. The rocky shoreline made it easy for sailors to get shipwrecked trying to reach land.

On their voyage down the western coast, Dias and his crew were blown far from shore by a terrible storm that lasted for two weeks.

They could no longer see land. When the storm was over, they headed east, but they were still surrounded by water. So they turned north. Finally, they saw land. The storm had ended up sending them right around the tip of Africa! Now the Portuguese realized that the Atlantic and Indian Oceans were connected. Dias very much wanted to continue on to India, but his crew begged him to return home. Tired and scared, they had had enough.

On their way back, Dias and his crew saw the most southwestern point of Africa. He named it the Cape of Storms. (King John II later changed the name to the Cape of Good Hope.) They returned home sixteen months after they had left, without any celebration.

Twelve years later, Dias returned to sea on a trip to India with Pedro Álvares Cabral. But Dias and his entire crew drowned in an unexpected storm near that very cape. So much for glory!

CHAPTER 4
A New Player: Christopher Columbus

An Italian navigator had an idea that had been kicking around for a long time. His name was Christopher Columbus. He thought that sailing around Africa to reach Asia wasn't the shortest or easiest way to get to the Indies. Columbus believed he had a better plan—sailing west from Portugal, straight across the Atlantic.

Columbus first approached King John II of Portugal because he had already paid for many voyages of exploration. But Bartholomeu Dias had already proven that going around Africa could work. The king was not interested in trying a new route, especially one that he believed would take longer.

So Columbus next turned to King Ferdinand and Queen Isabella of Spain. And they were

interested. They didn't want their neighbor
Portugal becoming too rich and powerful. But
Ferdinand and Isabella were involved in a war
in southern Spain and didn't have the money for
Columbus.

For six years, they kept putting him off. Then finally, in 1492, they were able to pay for his voyage. Not only did they provide money, they gave Columbus the title Grand Admiral of the Ocean Sea. The king and queen were excited about the possibility of riches and also about converting people to Christianity.

Niña   *Pinta*

In August, Columbus set sail from Spain with three ships—the *Niña*, the *Pinta*, and the *Santa María*. He chose to captain the *Santa María*, probably because it was a carrack, the largest, widest, and most comfortable of the three ships. It was slower, however, than the *Niña* and *Pinta*, which were smaller and faster caravels.

Santa María

There were eighty-six sailors on the three ships. Although Columbus expected the trip to take three weeks, he packed enough food for one year. There were barrels of water, casks of wine, flour to make biscuits called hardtack (as pleasant to eat as it sounds), dried beef and pork, salted fish, and dried peas and beans to eat.

Life aboard the ships was exhausting and uncomfortable. The work was hard. The food was bad and often had maggots in it. Also, it wasn't easy to get a good night's sleep because sailors slept on deck regardless of the weather.

There were many dangers at sea. Some were imaginary—sea monsters that would attack ships, mermaids who would lure sailors to crash into the rocks with their beautiful songs. But other dangers were real. Sudden storms. Accidents like

getting caught in the rigging. Harsh punishments for breaking the captain's rules. Shipworms that ate holes in a ship's hull. Lice, fleas, and rats to plague the sailors. Bad water to make them sick. And a mysterious disease called scurvy.

Scurvy

When sailors had scurvy, their gums would swell and their teeth would fall out. Healed wounds would reopen. Many died. It was thought that scurvy was contagious. But it wasn't. Much later, it was discovered that scurvy was caused by a lack of vitamin C. If the sailors had had oranges or grapefruit or lemons to eat, they wouldn't have fallen sick with scurvy. Unfortunately, none of those fruits grew in Europe at that time.

The trip was taking much longer than Columbus had told the crew. The sailors were getting scared. They began to grumble. Columbus was worried about a mutiny. A mutiny is when members of a crew all band together, make the captain their prisoner, and take over the ship.

Columbus came up with a clever way to trick his crew and avoid a mutiny. He kept two logs.

One had all false entries. Each day, the log said the ships had sailed only a few miles. Columbus let the crew see this log. The men were less scared, thinking they had not traveled very far. In the other, secret log, Columbus wrote down the real distances. In truth, the journey was much longer than Columbus had expected.

According to Columbus's log, on the night of October 11 he saw a light—a tiny one— in the distance. He wrote, "At two hours after midnight the land appeared, from which we were about two leagues distant." They had arrived!

Because no one had any idea that there were continents between Europe and Asia, Columbus was certain he had reached the Indies. He was wrong. The ships had arrived at a small island in the Bahamas.

Columbus named the island San Salvador and claimed it for Spain. He next sailed to Cuba, and then Hispaniola, certain it was Cipango (Japan). He and his crew discovered several Native tribes, including the Tainos. Columbus called them "Indians" because he thought they were the people of the Indies.

The Native people were curious about these strange-looking sailors. They welcomed Columbus and his crew, bringing them food and water and giving them gold jewelry in exchange

for trinkets—like glass beads, strings of bells, and red wool hats.

Columbus was interested in finding more gold to bring back for the king and queen. (Plus he got to keep 10 percent of whatever riches he found.) He heard there was gold in the northern part of Hispaniola. So in December 1492, he set off in the *Santa María* in search of it.

In the early hours of Christmas morning, however, the *Santa María* hit a reef and sank. Columbus then needed more ships, and for them he had to return to Spain. The *Pinta*, however,

had been off exploring the area, and Columbus didn't know where the ship was. That left the *Niña*. There wasn't enough room for everyone aboard, so he had to leave thirty-nine crew members behind.

Who Got There First?

Christopher Columbus usually gets the credit for being the first European to set foot on North America. But if Leif Erikson could have spoken to Columbus, he might have said, "Been there, done that, five hundred years before you." Leif Erikson was a Viking. In about the year 1000, he sailed west from Greenland and in time landed in Canada. He named the area "Vinland" after the wild grapes growing on vines there. He started a settlement and stayed for a year before returning home. Other Vikings sailed there later and stayed for a few years.

The sailors built a shelter on Hispaniola out of the wreck and called it La Navidad ("Christmas" in Spanish).

Two days, later, the *Pinta* showed up. Columbus brought a small amount of gold, spices, parrots, and had captured some Taino people for the king and queen. The two ships set off but got separated again because of a terrible storm.

Both, however, made it back to Spain. Although
Columbus didn't bring back much treasure, there
was much celebrating when he returned. He had
made it all the way to the Indies after all!

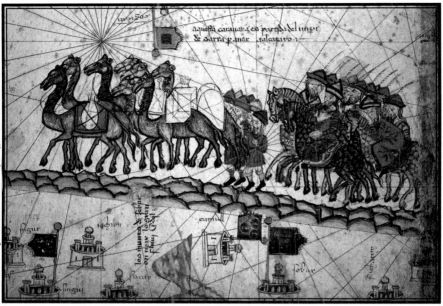

Fourteenth-century map showing Marco Polo on his way to Cathay (China)

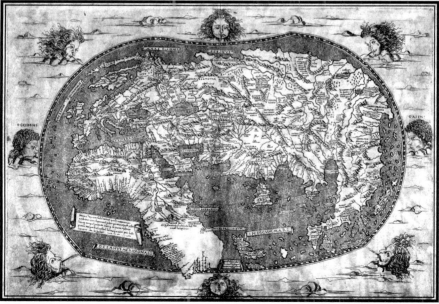

Fifteenth-century world map

our sauoir la pure uerite des diuses regions
dou mode · lisiez ou faciez lire cest liure · z y
uerrez les grinz merueilles qui isont es-
tes · z les plus grz miuoilles dou siecle · q
de la grit armenie de pse z des tarptars.
z dynde z de maintes autres prouinces
li come nre liures nos contera tout p ordene apteint.
de ce q messires martpol cytoiens deuenisse raconte
pour ce qil les uit · mais aucunes choses ya q il ne
uit pas · Et porce mettons nos les choses uehues p
ueues · Et les entendues por entendues · a ce q nre liure
soit bon z uentiauble · Car saichiez q puis ycele houre q
nre sires dex forma adan nre pmier pere · ne fu onques
nus hons de nule generacion qui tant seust necerchat
des diuses pties dou monde z des grz miuoilles come
tex maistres martpol fist · Et por ce pensa q mout seroit
grinz maus sil ne tacoit mattre en escrit ce quil auoit z
ueu z oy puerite · por ce q les genz qui ne lont ueu ne oy
le saichent p ce liure · Et si demoura por sauoir en ces
diuses pties p lespace de · xxvi · anz · Le quel liure ensi
come il estoit en la chartre de genues · il fist retralire p
ordene a monsr rusta pyssan qui en cele meisme pson estoit au tens q li incarnacions de ihucrist corroit sum
onl · cc · iiij · z · xviij · anz · Cy pmiers chapitres est
coment li dui frere se pert tout ·

l fu uoirs que au tens que baudoins estoit empareres de
costantinoble · ce fu lan de lincarnacion ihucrist · m · cc ·
· l · iiij · auoit nicholaus pol qui estoit peres mons mart ·

Da. Octauus/

Discoveries Monument with Prince Henry the Navigator
(front figure) in Lisbon, Portugal

Portuguese caravel sails on the Tagus River, 2020

Spanish monument of Queen Isabella and Christopher Columbus

Cape of Good Hope in South Africa

Replicas of Columbus's ships, the *Niña*, the *Pinta*, and the *Santa María*

Taino Arawak people performing in Cuba

Magellanic penguins on Magdalena Island
in the Strait of Magellan, southern Chile

Statue of Juan Ponce de León in Miami, Florida

Ruins of the ancient city of Tenochtitlán, in Mexico City

Inca ruins outside Cuzco, Peru

The Northwest Passage that Giovanni da Verrazzano
searched for but never found

Mosaic outside a church in Mexico City showing
Montezuma II meeting Hernán Cortés

Tomb of Portuguese explorer Vasco da Gama

In September 1493, Christopher Columbus set off from Spain to return to Hispaniola and the crew members he had left behind. This time he had an impressive fleet of seventeen ships with about 1,500 men aboard, including Columbus's brother Diego. (Another brother, Bartholomew, met up with them later.) They were going to start a settlement. Columbus brought cattle, horses, and dogs as well as seeds to plant.

The Treaty of Tordesillas

At this time, the New World—which really wasn't new at all—"belonged" to Spain and Portugal. At least, that's how the two countries saw it.

But neither Spain nor Portugal wanted the other to become the more powerful country. So what did they do? They divided up the world between them. They did this through a treaty (a contract between countries).

On June 7, 1494, with the help of Pope Alexander VI, they signed the Treaty of Tordesillas. It stated that everything west of the Cape Verde Islands (off the west coast of Africa) belonged to Spain, and everything east belonged to Portugal. Also, Spain was allowed to sail into Portugal's zone, provided the Spanish ships did no exploring. The fate of the millions of people who

already lived in these places never came up.
Why would it have? The Europeans considered them
savages, not people worthy of consideration.

This was the beginning of what historians have come to call the Columbian Exchange. Named after Christopher Columbus, it describes the "swaps" between Europe and the New World that resulted from the voyages of exploration. There were exchanges of foods, animals, and ideas. Europe was introduced to things like tomatoes, potatoes, and corn. Cacao and tobacco. The New World was introduced to horses, pigs, sugarcane, apples, wheat, and rice, as well as other animals and goods.

The Columbian Exchange also brought slavery and disease to the New World, destroying the lives of millions.

New Diseases

The diseases that the Europeans brought to the New World included smallpox, whooping cough, measles, scarlet fever, and mumps. The Native people had no immunity against them. It is estimated that 90 percent of the Native population was wiped out by 1600, mostly by disease.

On arriving at La Navidad on Hispaniola in late November 1493, Columbus and the crew found that the thirty-nine men who had stayed behind were all dead. Every single one. The men had grown tired of fending for themselves and had tried to steal from the Tainos. The Native people fought back.

Did this stop Columbus from starting another settlement? No. He decided to call it La Isabela after the queen. But things did not go well. Instead of building houses and planting crops, the Spaniards seemed much more interested in looking for gold. Not used to the humid, tropical climate, many got sick and died. Columbus got sick, too. A hurricane struck and all the ships were damaged, some completely destroyed.

Frustrated by the lack of gold, Columbus told the Tainos that they had to give him a certain amount of gold every three months. It was an impossible demand. There just wasn't that much gold on Hispaniola.

Columbus decided he would impress the king and queen another way. He enslaved five hundred people and sent them back to Spain. He thought this would please the queen. But it didn't. Not at all. Queen Isabella wanted the people sent back home. Because Hispaniola then belonged to Spain, the queen considered the Native people Spaniards—and because they were her subjects,

she said, they should be free. Converting people to the Christian religion was fine with her. Enslaving them, however, was not.

So far, the king and queen were disappointed with the results of Columbus's voyages. Yet somehow, he convinced them to let him make a third trip, in 1498. Along the way, he claimed Venezuela for Spain. Once again, Columbus had no idea where he really was. He thought he had come upon the Garden of Eden. He was sure he would find gold there—lots of it—because he believed that the legendary mines of King Solomon mentioned in the Bible were nearby. Once again, he was wrong.

Meanwhile, on Hispaniola, both the Tainos and the Spaniards were in revolt against the Columbus brothers, Diego and Bartholomew. The brothers were quick to dole out harsh punishments. Enslaving people, cutting off their noses and ears, hanging them.

Instead of settling things, Columbus's arrival only made the situation worse. Things were so bad that a judge was sent from Spain, and all three of the Columbus brothers were sent home to Spain in chains in 1500.

Amazingly, this was not the end of Christopher Columbus's career as an explorer. The king and queen released him, and sent him on a fourth voyage in 1502. But this time he was forbidden to return to Hispaniola and was no longer to be called the Great Admiral of the Ocean Sea.

His job was to find an entrance into the Indian Ocean from Cuba (which Columbus still insisted was Cathay). Of course there wasn't one, and at a certain point he gave up. He began to search for gold again, but that didn't work out, either. A hurricane damaged his ship, and he and his crew were marooned in Jamaica for one year.

They were finally rescued in 1504 by the new governor of Hispaniola. Columbus was quite ill and was sent back to Spain for the last time. He died there in 1506, never realizing he had landed in a part of the world until then unknown to Europeans—the Americas.

Amerigo Vespucci (1454?–1512)

It was a friend of Christopher Columbus's, an Italian explorer from the city-state of Florence, who realized that Columbus had reached a new continent. His name was Amerigo Vespucci. Through his exploration of the northern coast of South America, Vespucci became convinced that this was not the Indies but a new world. A German mapmaker read Vespucci's notes on the voyage and mistakenly named the New World "America" after him.

Columbus's mistake was a real jackpot for the Europeans. The stores of gold that Columbus had been searching for would soon be found. The Europeans had learned that a land full of riches and Native people to convert to Christianity lay between Europe and Asia. The explorers didn't need to reach China. They would conquer the New World instead.

CHAPTER 5
Things Get Spicy for Portugal

It wasn't until eight years after Bartholomeu Dias's 1487 voyage that the Portuguese sent ships to try to reach India again. By 1495, King John II was dead. King Manuel I was on the throne. In July 1497, he provided Vasco da Gama (say: VAS-co duh GAH-ma) and his crew with four ships.

Vasco da Gama

They did manage to sail from Lisbon around the southern tip of Africa, up the eastern coast, and across the Indian Ocean to Calicut, India, a trading center run by Muslims. They arrived in May 1498.

Yes, da Gama made it. But it was a terrible trip, taking more than ten months. The crew was attacked along the African coast, and many developed scurvy. So many died of the disease (including da Gama's brother Paolo) that they had to burn down one of the boats because there weren't enough men left to sail it.

And da Gama didn't return to Portugal with riches. The goods he had brought to trade in Calicut were not impressive. So he was able to obtain only a small amount of spices in return. Even so, King Manuel was pleased. Finally, there was a direct sea route to India!

Vasco da Gama with the ruler of Calicut

With the new route mapped, King Manuel wanted to take over the spice trade from the Muslims and the Italians who worked with them. He wanted Portugal to own this business. In

March 1500, he sent Pedro Álvares Cabral and a fleet of thirteen ships to do just that.

But Cabral's voyage took him to an unexpected spot. On the way down the western coast of Africa, Cabral headed west to take advantage of the northwest trade winds. But he didn't mean to head as far west as he did. He ended up sailing to Brazil! He claimed it for Portugal.

After a short stay, Cabral headed east to
resume his voyage to India. But as the fleet
rounded the Cape of Good Hope at the
southern tip of Africa, a storm struck. Four
ships were sunk. All the sailors on them died,

including Bartholomeu Dias, who was on the voyage.

When the remaining ships made it to Calicut, they were better received by the ruler. The king of Portugal had sent more suitable gifts, and Cabral was rewarded with trading rights.

Were the Muslim traders in Calicut pleased with this new development? Oh no. They attacked and killed many Portuguese. Cabral and his men responded by burning ten Muslim ships with six hundred sailors aboard, then attacking the city. Cabral next sailed south to the port of Cochin and signed a trade treaty there. Portugal had finally broken into the spice trade.

In 1502, King Manuel sent Vasco da Gama back to India with twenty ships. He wanted to show the Muslims (and the Italians) who was boss. When da Gama's fleet reached the eastern coast of Africa, they started attacking

Muslim trading ports. They even burned a ship full of Muslims returning from a pilgrimage (a religious journey) to Mecca.

Portugal was at war with the Muslim traders for several years. But the Portuguese had better ships and more of them, too. By 1511, Portugal had complete control of the spice route to the east.

CHAPTER 6
All the Way Around the Globe

Once there was a much clearer idea of what the world actually looked like, a Portuguese explorer wanted to sail all the way around it. His name was Ferdinand Magellan, and by sailing west, he hoped to reach the Spice Islands. He was certain that was possible. He'd sail from Spain to South America and continue down its  eastern coast. He had heard there was a strait (a narrow waterway that connects two big bodies of water) toward the southern part of the continent (the area that is now Chile). The route would be safer and quicker than sailing all the way around the tip of South America, around Cape Horn. The sea there was stormy, with strong currents and many icebergs.

King Manuel of Portugal had no interest in this expedition. So, like Columbus before him, Magellan next tried seeking help from Spain. And yes! He convinced King Charles I (the grandson of King Ferdinand and Queen Isabella) to sponsor the voyage. The young king provided him with 270 men and five ships—

Magellan's five ships

the *Santiago, San Antonio, Conception, Trinidad,* and *Victoria.* Magellan was the captain of the *Trinidad.*

It was September 1519 when Magellan departed Spain, leaving behind his wife and their baby son. The voyage got off to a terrible start. Stopping in the Canary Islands, Magellan learned three of his captains intended to mutiny and kill him. And when King Manuel discovered that Spain had financed the voyage, he became furious and sent Portuguese ships after Magellan.

But the captain kept his cool. Magellan changed his route to avoid being caught by the Portuguese ships. And he kept an eye on the three mutinous captains.

The Atlantic crossing took two weeks. They landed in Brazil, where they got fresh water and food and converted some of the Native people. From there, they began to head south in the direction of Antarctica. The weather got colder and stormier. They saw strange creatures including penguins and sea lions.

In late March 1520, since winter was coming (in the Southern Hemisphere winter is from June to August), they decided to stop in the area known as Patagonia (now part of both Chile and Argentina). On Easter Sunday, the three captains made their move. They tried to mutiny. But thanks to the warning he had received while in the Canary Islands, Magellan was prepared. Two of the captains were killed, and the third was left behind in Patagonia.

While the rest of the crew members were repairing the ships, Magellan sent the *Santiago* ahead to find the strait. Unfortunately, the vessel was shipwrecked in a storm, although two crew members were able to make it back to Patagonia— and eventually, the rest of the crew was rescued.

In August, they renewed the search for the strait. They finally found it in October. But it was such a cold, rough, long passage that the crew of the *San Antonio* decided enough was enough. They turned around and began the long trip back to Spain. There were only three ships left.

After a month in the winding, frigid strait, they came out into the ocean that Balboa had named the South Sea, seven years earlier. Magellan renamed it *Mar Pacifico*—"the Pacific"—because the waters were so calm. (*Pacific* means "peaceful." And the Pacific Ocean is not particularly calm, so that tells you how stormy it was in the strait named for him!) Magellan was the first European to sail from the Atlantic to the Pacific. But there was still so far to go. Rats on board ate their food, and the starving sailors had to eat sawdust and pieces of leather to survive.

With a bit of much-needed luck, they spotted land on March 6, 1521. They landed on Guam, an island east of the Philippines, where they got food and fresh water. Magellan sailed on and claimed the Philippines for  Spain. There, in Cebu City, he made friends with (and converted) a group of Native people. The leader asked for Magellan's help fighting against a rival from nearby Mactan. Magellan agreed. It was a bad decision. A really bad decision. During the battle in late April, Magellan was shot by a poison arrow, then finished off by several spears. Magellan was only halfway through his round-the-world trip.

As for the supposedly friendly island ruler, a few days later he tricked thirty of the remaining crew members into coming to a feast.

There was a fancy meal and lots of wine to drink. Then, right after the dinner, Magellan's men were attacked and killed. Those who survived were enslaved.

After the battle, there were about 115 men left, not enough to man three vessels. They had to burn the *Conception*. On November 8, 1521, they finally reached the Spice Islands. They traded for two boatloads full of cloves and other spices. Was that the end of all the trouble?

No. As they left to return to Spain, the *Trinidad* began to leak and had to stay behind for repairs. Then it was captured and destroyed by the Portuguese, who had been sent by the king to find Magellan.

In September 1522, three years after the voyage began, the *Victoria* returned to Spain loaded with spices but with just 18 of the original 271 men aboard. And although Magellan is known as being the first man to circumnavigate (sail all around) the world, he never actually completed the journey himself.

The world turned out to be much bigger than people had thought. Oceans were vaster. Even so, at last it had been proven that it was possible to sail all the way around it.

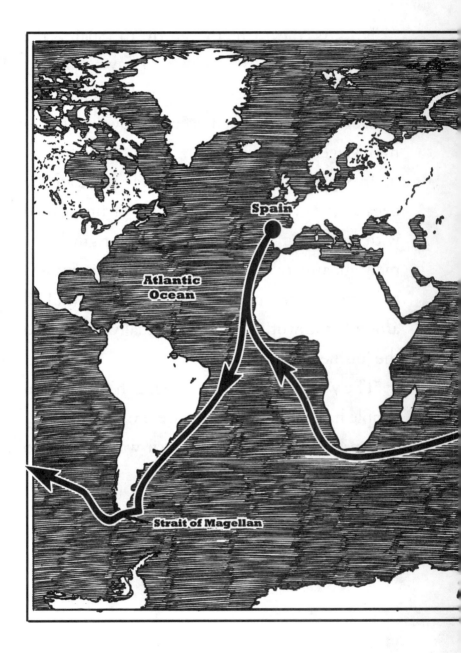

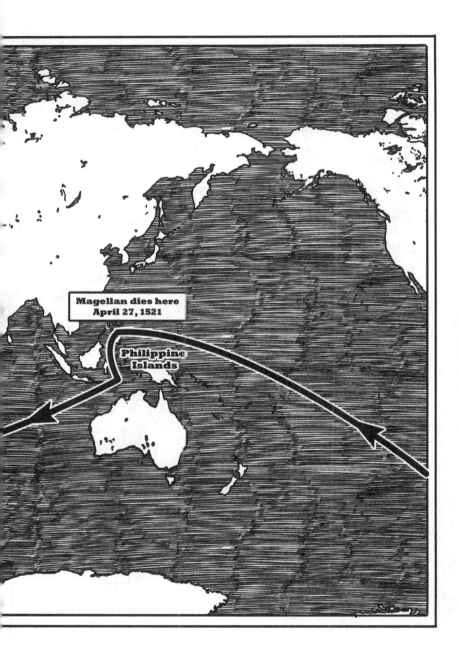

The Panama Canal

It wasn't until 1914 that a man-made waterway was built to connect the Atlantic and Pacific Oceans. It is called the Panama Canal and goes across the Isthmus of Panama (explored by Vasco Núñez de Balboa in 1513). This makes the trip from the Atlantic to the Pacific eight thousand miles shorter than by sailing around Cape Horn at the tip of South America.

CHAPTER 7
A New Kind of Explorer

Spain outpaced Portugal in exploration in the 1500s. There was a new kind of explorer. They were men who wanted to conquer the ancient civilizations they came in contact with and collect their bounties of gold, silver, and jewels. In Spanish, they were called *conquistadores*; in English, *conquistadors* (say: kuhn-KEE-stuh-dors).

Juan Ponce de León is probably best known for being the first European to explore Florida, in April 1513. He named it La Florida, which means "full of flowers." It is said that he did so while searching for the so-called

Juan Ponce de León

Fountain of Youth (a spring that granted eternal youth to those who drank from it), but that is likely a made-up story. Ponce de León was an accomplished explorer, engineer, and leader. He began his career in 1493 on Christopher Columbus's second voyage. Ten years later, he was named governor of a settlement on Hispaniola. He was sent to Puerto Rico in 1508 to find gold, and did. There he founded a settlement in the area that is present-day San Juan, the capital of Puerto Rico.

Ponce de León distinguished himself further when, in 1516, he became the first European to set foot in Mexico. In fact, it was by using de León's sea chart that Hernán Cortés, another conquistador, was able to reach Mexico in 1519. Once there, he would wipe out the Aztecs at the height of their power.

The Aztec empire, located in what is now central and southern Mexico, was large, rich,

and powerful. It was a collection of hundreds
of city-states that surrounded the main city of
Tenochtitlán (say: teh-NOTCH-teet-LAHN),
which was established in about 1325. The city

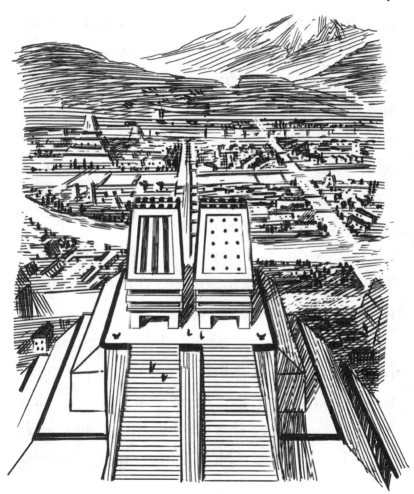

was spread over several islands in the middle of Lake Texcoco.

At least two hundred thousand people lived in Tenochtitlán alone. The society was divided into the noble class and the commoners. There were enslaved people, mostly people who had been conquered. It had a well-trained military and schools. Like many ancient civilizations, the Aztecs practiced human sacrifice as part of their religion. They farmed many different kinds of crops, and also hunted and fished. They grew cotton and wove beautiful fabric. They had a calendar with 365 days and a writing system. There were markets for trading that drew tens of thousands of people.

Cortés had heard about this rich empire in Mexico. He was thrilled when the governor of Cuba asked him to explore Mexico's interior. Then the governor changed his mind, but Cortés didn't care. He assembled an army of six hundred men and sailed to Veracruz, a city on the Gulf of Mexico. To make sure that his men could not turn back once they arrived, he sank his own ships.

What lay ahead was a months-long march through the jungle to reach Tenochtitlán. Cortés's army had guns and horses, which the Native people had never seen before. Along the way, Cortés met Native people who resented the Aztec leader. His name was Montezuma II, and the Native people had to pay tribute to him. They didn't like that. So Cortés convinced them to join his army.

The army, which had grown to at least sixteen hundred men, arrived in Tenochtitlán in November 1519. Montezuma II welcomed Cortés and gave him gifts of gold.

The story goes that when Montezuma asked Cortés why he loved gold so much, the Spaniard responded, "We suffer from a disease that only gold can cure." Shortly afterward, he arrested Montezuma and held him hostage. Cortés then ruled Tenochtitlán and stockpiled gold.

Cortés couldn't help but be impressed by

the Aztec city. In a letter to the king of Spain, he described the many public squares with their lively markets. There were medicine shops, barber shops, and restaurants. "Everything that can be found throughout the whole country is sold in the markets," he wrote.

Cortés discovered that the governor of Cuba

Pedro de Alvarado

had sent men after him. He gathered some of his army and left Tenochtitlán to fight them. He left his second-in-command, the hotheaded Pedro de Alvarado, in charge.

Cortés was able to fight the governor's men and win. The surviving men had no choice but to join Cortés's army. Meanwhile, in Tenochtitlán, Pedro de Alvarado decided to murder thousands of Aztecs. They were gathered for an important feast day and made easy targets for the Spaniards.

Cortés returned to find the Aztecs in full rebellion. In the chaos, Montezuma was killed (no one is sure if he was killed by the Spanish or his own people). Cortés realized he was outnumbered. He and his men escaped from Tenochtitlán on June 30, during what is called Noche Triste ("Sad Night"). Sad for Cortés, that is. Half of his men were killed, and the treasure he had plundered was lost.

But Cortés was not finished with the Aztecs.

He returned to Tenochtitlán soon after. The Aztecs were weakened. Many were suffering from smallpox, brought by the Spanish. Cortés cut off their food and water, and they were defeated by August 1521. The Aztec empire was renamed New Spain, and in 1522, Cortés became the governor. Several years later he was removed and sent back to Spain.

In less than two years, Cortés had defeated a thriving, long-standing civilization. And more than five hundred years later, the most common language spoken in Mexico is Spanish.

CHAPTER 8
The Inca

A distant relative of Hernán Cortés, Francisco Pizarro, would also destroy an entire civilization out of sheer greediness.

Francisco Pizarro

Pizarro, the former mayor of Panama City, had heard of the rich Inca empire located high in the Andes Mountains. It was a difficult place to reach, and it took three attempts over several years by Pizarro and his fellow conquistador Diego de Almagro to find it.

The Incas were as impressive as the Aztecs. The empire, with its capital called Cuzco,

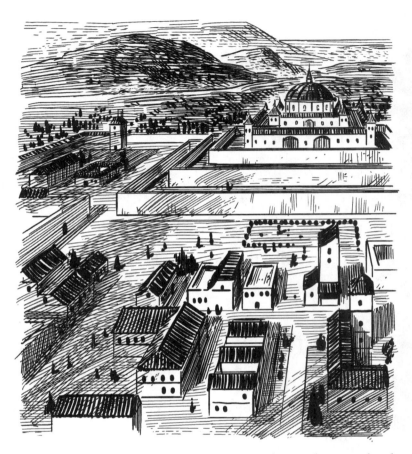

consisted of twelve million people and stretched
for two thousand miles from north to south. They
had a large army, used abacuses for complicated
math, collected taxes, irrigated their crops,
domesticated llamas for transportation, and grew

a strange root vegetable (potatoes) that over time would become part of most peoples' diets in Europe. As with the Aztecs, their religion included human sacrifice. The Incas also had built 15,500 miles of roads.

Pizarro and Almagro's timing could not have been better. It was 1532 and Huayna Capac (say: WHY-na ka-pak), the Incan leader, had recently died. His two sons, Atahuallpa (say: AT-uh-WAAL-puh) and Huascar (say: WAS-kar), each wanted to rule. So Atahuallpa started a civil war and killed his half brother.

Though greatly outnumbered (he had only 180 men), Pizzaro launched a surprise attack on Atahuallpa. Pizzaro and his men killed thousands of Incas that day. Atahuallpa was captured and held for eight months. Pizarro said he'd set the ruler free if he gave over gold and silver—enough to fill a room. Atahuallpa agreed, but Pizarro killed him anyway.

Pizarro took over the Inca empire, moving the capital to the coast of the Pacific and calling it Lima. Diego Almagro was not happy. The conquistadors were rough men, and there was no loyalty or friendship between them. Later, when the Incas recaptured Cuzco from Pizarro's brothers, Almagro stepped in with his own army and took the city for himself. To get back at him, Pizarro had Almagro captured, imprisoned, and killed. Three years later, Diego, Almagro's son, decided to avenge his father's death. In June 1541, he stabbed Pizarro to death. Legend has it that Pizarro, who was known as a very religious man, fell to the ground and drew a cross on the floor in his own blood and kissed it before he died. Diego would be executed a year later.

The bloody deeds of Pizarro and Cortés inspired other conquistadors to strike out in search of their own jackpots. Fortunes—and lives—were lost in the pursuit. These men didn't get any of the glory they were looking for. Or the gold.

For centuries, conquistadors were portrayed in history books as heroes, risking their very lives as they bravely set out to explore unknown lands. But more recently, their cruel behavior and disregard for the people, animals, and lands they conquered has come to light, painting a truer portrait.

CHAPTER 9
The Search for the Northwest Passage

With Spain and Portugal grabbing so much of the "New World," what was left for other countries to explore and claim as theirs? Well, perhaps there was yet another route to the Indies. Some were convinced that the Indies could be

Northwest Passage through the Arctic Ocean

reached by what came to be called the Northwest Passage. This meant traveling from the Atlantic to the Pacific by sailing through the Arctic Ocean near the North Pole.

In 1524, Francis I, the king of France, decided to fund a voyage. He chose an Italian explorer named Giovanni da Verrazzano (say: joh-VAHN-nee dah VER-uh-ZAA-no) to lead it.

Verrazzano thought he might be able to find an outlet from the Atlantic to the Pacific through North America. But he never found it. So he ended up exploring the eastern coast of North America.

In a letter to the king in July 1524, Verrazzano described a pleasant experience his crew had with some Native people. (They were in what is present-day North Carolina.) A young sailor who was swimming to shore with trinkets for the Native people nearly drowned. The Native people carried him to safety and made a huge fire to keep him warm. After remaining with them for a while, the sailor had regained his strength, and he showed by hand signals that he wanted to return to the ship. So they accompanied him back to his ship, holding him close and embracing him.

Giovanni da Verrazzano would not be so lucky as that young sailor. In 1528, he set out on his third voyage to find a route to Asia. His brother joined him. They ventured into the Carribean Sea and Verrazzano and a few of the crew members decided to explore a small island. They were captured, killed, and eaten by cannibals while Verrazzano's brother and the rest of the crew helplessly watched from the ship.

England was also interested in finding a new route to the Indies. In 1497 and 1498, King Henry VII sent an explorer named John Cabot (known as Giovanni Caboto in his native Italy) on a search for the Northwest Passage. Cabot didn't find it, but he landed in Newfoundland in 1497, claiming North America for England, which led to England later claiming Canada. He disappeared during his next trip, without a trace.

Henry Hudson

More than a hundred years later, in 1610, the English explorer and navigator Henry Hudson, his son John, and a crew of twenty-three men set sail from London across the Atlantic in a ship called the *Discovery*. This would be his second attempt to find the Northwest Passage. (His first attempt had been for the Dutch East India Company, which made England mad. So he agreed to explore for England on his next trip.)

Hudson sailed to Iceland and around Greenland. The *Discovery* went through a strait (which would later be named Hudson Strait) and entered a bay (Hudson Bay). Hudson and his crew then headed south and began to search for the passage but became stuck in the ice in James Bay. The winter was brutal. Tempers flared, and the crew accused Hudson of hiding food.

Once spring came, Hudson wanted to continue the search for the passage. But members of the the crew had had enough. They wanted to return to England. They forced Hudson, his son, and seven sick sailors into a rowboat. Hudson was able to keep up with the ship for several days, then fell behind. He and the others in the boat were never seen again.

Explorers would search for two hundred years more for the elusive Northwest Passage. They failed because the waters around the Arctic Islands froze up in the winter, delaying exploration.

It would not be until 1906 that the Northwest Passage was at last navigated. Roald Amundsen, a Norwegian explorer, became the first to do so. Now, because of global warming, the ice caps in the Arctic Circle are melting at a much faster rate than they used to. And the melting starts earlier in the year. This is terrible for the planet; sailing via the Northwest Passage, however, can be done with greater ease.

CHAPTER 10
The Age of Exploration: A Lasting Impact

Voyaging into unknown parts of the world was a dangerous business. But certain men were willing to take the chance in the hope of finding riches and fame.

But most of the explorers did not become rich or powerful. As with Vasco Núñez de Balboa, who ended up with his head on a spike, their stories did not end well. Many drowned, were marooned, or remained penniless and in disgrace while their sponsors received the bounty of their efforts—riches, new territories, and new people to rule.

This all came at a terrible cost to the original inhabitants of the lands being explored. In the explorers' quest for gold, God, and glory, the

Native peoples were attacked, abused, enslaved, and murdered. New diseases such as measles and smallpox were introduced, decimating the vulnerable Native populations. Fifty-six million Native people were wiped out in one hundred years. And more than twelve million African people were stolen from their families and brought to the New World between 1525 and when slavery was abolished.

The Age of Exploration used to be known as the Age of Discovery. But how could these lands be "discovered" when people had already been living on them for thousands of years? For them, this period in time could more accurately be called the Age of Invasion.

Timeline of the Age of Exploration

1000 —	Leif Erikson is first European in North America
1271 —	Marco Polo, his father, and his uncle set out for China
1419–1450 —	Prince Henry the Navigator funds expeditions to Africa
1434 —	Gil Eanes sails past Cape Bojador
1488 —	Bartholomeu Dias finds sea route around Africa's southern coast
1492 —	Christopher Columbus's first voyage
1498 —	Vasco da Gama reaches India
1501 —	Amerigo Vespucci determines that Columbus found the New World
1513 —	Vasco Núñez de Balboa is first European to see the Pacific Ocean
1516 —	Ponce de León is first European to set foot in Mexico
1521 —	Hernán Cortés conquers the Aztecs
1522 —	Ferdinand Magellan's ship is first to sail around world
1524 —	Giovanni da Verrazzano explores the northeastern coast of North America
1532 —	Francisco Pizarro conquers the Inca
1610 —	Henry Hudson begins second trip to find the Northwest Passage

Timeline of the World

1206 —	Genghis Khan becomes the ruler of the Mongol empire
1231 —	The Medieval Inquisition begins
1280 —	Gunpowder is invented
1325 —	Tenochitilán founded
—	The Renaissance begins in Italy
1337 —	The Hundred Years' War begins
1346 —	The bubonic plague reaches Europe
1368 —	The Ming Dynasty begins
1421 —	Beijing becomes the official capital of China
1429 —	Joan of Arc leads the French army against the English
1450 —	The printing press is perfected
1452 —	Leonardo da Vinci is born
1475 —	Michelangelo is born
1488 —	The Great Wall of China is rebuilt
1507 —	The New World is named "America" on map
1517 —	The Protestant Reformation begins
1564 —	Shakespeare is born
1600 —	British East India Company is formed
1602 —	Dutch East India Company is formed
1610 —	Galileo Galilei discovers Jupiter's moons and Saturn

Bibliography

*Books for young readers

Ames, Glenn Joseph. *The Globe Encompassed: The Age of European Discovery, 1500–1700*. Upper Saddle River, NJ: Pearson Prentice Hall, 2008.

Bedini, Silvio A., ed. *The Christopher Columbus Encyclopedia*. New York: Simon & Schuster, 1992.

Bergreen, Laurence. *Over the Edge of the World: Magellan's Terrifying Circumnavigation of the Globe*. New York: Morrow, 2003.

Boorstin, Daniel J. *The Discoverers*. New York: Random House, 1983.

*Everett, Felicity, and Struan Reid. *The Usborne Book of Explorers*. London: Usborne Publishing Ltd., 1991.

*Fritz, Jean. *Around the World in a Hundred Years: From Henry the Navigator to Magellan*. New York: Puffin Books, 1998.

Nicolle, David. *The Portuguese in the Age of Discovery c. 1340–1665*. Oxford, UK: Osprey Publishing Ltd, 2012.

Parry, J. H. *The Age of Reconnaissance: Discovery, Exploration, and Settlement 1450 to 1650*. Berkeley: University of California Press, 1981.

PBS. "The Story of . . . Smallpox—and other Deadly Eurasian
    Germs." *Guns, Germs, and Steel*. https://www.pbs.org/
    gunsgermssteel/variables/smallpox.html.

Pletcher, Kenneth, ed. *The Britannica Guide to Explorers and
    Explorations That Changed the Modern World*.
    New York: Encyclopedia Britannica Educational Publishing,
    2010.

*Starkey, Dinah. *Scholastic Atlas of Exploration*. New York:
    Scholastic Reference, 1993.

Wroth, Lawrence C., ed. "The Written Record of the Voyage of 1524
    of Giovanni da Verrazzano as recorded in a letter to Francis
    I, King of France." *The Voyages of Giovanni da Verrazzano,
    1524–1528*, 133–143. Translated by Susan Tarrow. New
    Haven: Yale University Press, 1970. http://www.columbia.
    edu/~lmg21/ash3002y/earlyac99/documents/verrazan.htm.

Website

marinersmuseum.org